The Butterfly Cycle

By Oxford Scientific Films

Photographs by Dr. John Cooke

G. P. Putnam's Sons New York

First American Edition 1977
Text Copyright © 1976 by Nature's Way/G. Whizzard Publications Ltd.
Photographs © 1976 by Oxford Scientific Films Ltd.
All rights reserved.
Printed by Toppan Printing Co. Singapore

Library of Congress Cataloging in Publication Data
Main entry on title: The Butterfly cycle.
SUMMARY: Text and photographs follow the life cycle of a butterfly
from egg through larva and pupa stages to adulthood.
1. Butterflies—juvenile literature. 2. Insects—
Metamorphosis—Juvenile literature.[1. Butterflies.
2. Insects—Metamorphosis] I. Cooke, John A L
II. Oxford Scientific Films.
QL544.2.B87 1977   595.7'89   76-45850
ISBN 0-399-20590-X   ISBN 0-399-61079-2 lib. bdg.

The Butterfly Cycle

The Cabbage White Butterfly (sometimes known as the Large White), like other members of the butterfly family, undergoes dramatic changes in shape and appearance during the course of its brief life.

There are basically four stages in the life cycle of a butterfly: first the egg; then the caterpillar or larva; next the chrysalis or pupa; and finally the adult butterfly.

The Cabbage White normally lays its eggs on the undersurface of the leaves of one of the Cabbage family — the plant best suited to the food needs of the caterpillar. Unlike many other butterflies, who deposit their eggs singly or in small batches, the Cabbage White lays its eggs in clusters of up to one hundred.

At first the eggs are pale yellow, with an attractively fluted surface; but as the caterpillar embryo develops, they slowly darken. After about ten days, the black head capsule of the caterpillar is clearly visible inside the egg. Those eggs that are infertile remain pale, and gradually shrivel up.

The caterpillar is now ready to hatch. It bites a hole in the top of the egg large enough to get its head through, then crawls out. All the eggs in a particular group hatch at about the same time. The caterpillars are tiny, measuring only some 3 mm (1/10 inch) in length. Their first meal usually consists of the now empty egg 'shell'.

At first, the young caterpillars remain together, feeding hungrily on the leaves of their foodplant; but eventually they disperse. Over a period of twenty or thirty days a caterpillar molts, or sheds, four times, increasing noticeably in size each time it sheds its skin.

The final molt produces a caterpillar approximately 38 mm (1½ inches) long. It continues to feed avidly, taking in as much food as possible to sustain it through the non-eating pupal stage which follows. The caterpillar is now fully grown, consisting of a head and thirteen segments — three thoracic (the area between the head and the abdomen) and ten abdominal.

The most striking feature of the caterpillar's head is its powerful mandibles or jaws, which enable it to bite through the leaves of the foodplant. These are in marked contrast to those of the adult butterfly, which are designed for sucking nectar. The antennae, later to become a key part of the butterfly's equipment, are still very small.

The caterpillar has six legs — one pair on each of the thoracic segments. Each leg has a single sharp claw on the end of it. In addition to these, on the abdomen, there are five pairs of leg-like limbs called prolegs. These have rows of tiny curved hooks on them, which are used to grip the surface of leaves.

Many caterpillars never reach the next stage of their development, falling prey to a variety of parasites and viral infections. But those that do survive leave the foodplant and select a suitable spot to pupate, or form its chrysalis, usually on a fence-post or tree-trunk. The caterpillar positions itself upright, spinning a silken pad onto which it hooks the lower part of its body. The upper part is secured by means of a fine girdle of silk which it weaves around itself.

The change from caterpillar to chrysalis, or pupa, starts with rhythmic movements of the body, as the blood pressure increases. The body swells, splitting the skin, which is then shed completely. And there, in place of the caterpillar, is the newly-emerged chrysalis.

On the outside of the chrysalis can be seen the outline and wing pattern of the developing butterfly. Inside, a great reconstruction process is taking place. Eventually, a perfect adult butterfly is ready to emerge. (There are two breeding periods a year, spring and autumn. In the spring, the pupal stage lasts for just two or three weeks; but the autumn brood remain in the chrysalis for up to eight months, emerging only when the warmer spring weather arrives.)

The butterfly breaks out of the chrysalis by thrusting and pushing from the inside. The chrysalis splits and the butterfly pulls itself free. Immediately, blood starts to flow through the veins, inflating the butterfly's wings to their full size. After a short rest, it is ready to fly.

The most noticeable difference between the male and female Cabbage Whites is the conspicuous black spots that the latter has on the upper part of her forewings — although in the normal resting position, with the wings together, this is not obvious.

The butterfly has a long tube-like tongue or proboscis, through which it sucks up the nectar on which it feeds (when it is resting, this is coiled up tightly beneath the head). The nectar merely provides enough energy for flight: the adult butterfly does not grow; its sole purpose is to reproduce, and it lives for just three or four weeks.

When the female is ready to mate, she opens her wings to display the black spots and raises her abdomen. This attracts the male, who, after hovering above for a while, flies down and mates with her. The two butterflies are joined at the tip of the abdomen, facing in opposite directions. The male squeezes the end of the female's abdomen with his claspers; fertilization is internal.

When ready to lay her eggs, the female settles on the edge of an appropriate leaf. Each egg is stuck individually to the undersurface of the leaf by means of a special secretion.

That done, the butterfly cycle begins all over again.

The photographs you are about to see show the butterfly and its environment magnified many, many times by the use of special cameras and techniques.

The Cabbage White lays its eggs . . . .

. . . . on the underneath part of the cabbage leaf.

After about ten days, the dark head of the caterpillar can be seen inside the egg.

Soon the caterpillar is ready to hatch. It bites a hole in the egg, and crawls out.

The caterpillars, which are now 3 mm (1/10 inch) long, eat non-stop.

They outgrow their skins four times in one month –
each time replacing the old skin with a new one.

The fully grown caterpillar, now about 38 mm (1½ inches) long, has 13 separate segments.

It has very strong jaws making it easy to bite through leaves.

On five of the last ten parts there are small leg-like limbs,
which it uses to hold onto leaves.

The caterpillar positions itself upright and spins a fine girdle of silk.

After a while it loses its skin and becomes a chrysalis.

cocoon

The butterfly breaks out of the chrysalis by pushing from the inside.

Now free of the chrysalis, its wings expand to full size – soon it is ready to fly.

This is the male Cabbage White butterfly.

The female has black spots on its forewings.

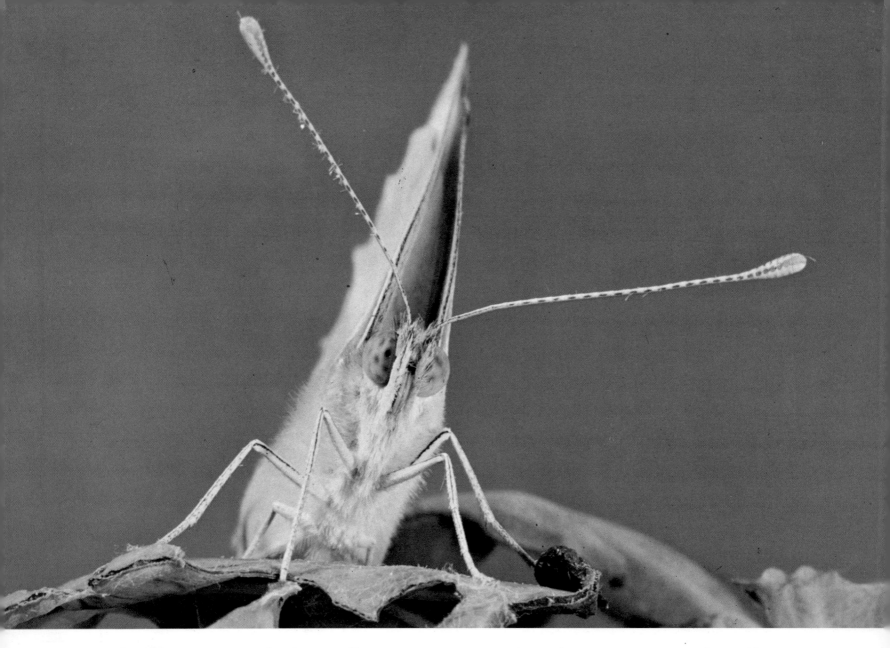

In the antennae the butterfly stores, among other things, its sense of smell.

Butterflies suck up nectar through their long tongues.

They exist only to reproduce, and soon they are mating.

The female lays her eggs, and the butterfly cycle starts again.

595.7
BUT

The Butterfly cycle

DATE			
APR 6 1976	AP 19 '91		
Feldman	JAN 8 1993		
MAY 8 '81	JA 22 '93		
SEP 29 '81	FEB 5 1993		
FEB 12 '82	FEB 26 1993		
MY 14 '82	MY 7 '93		
Feldman	FEB 3 1994		
Feldman	MAR 8 1994		
JAN 9, '87	APR 18 1994		
Feldman	APR 16 2002		
Feldman